Tangerine, Spark, and

Rainbow's Story

Written and Illustrated

by

Deborah James, M.A.

AuthorHouse™
1663 Liberty Drive
Bloomington, IN 47403
www.authorhouse.com
Phone: 833-262-8899

This book is printed on acid-free paper.

ISBN: 978-1-4685-4956-0 (sc)
ISBN: 979-8-8230-1744-2 (hc)
ISBN: 978-1-4772-3635-2 (e)

Library of Congress Control Number: 2012902068

Print information available on the last page.

Published by AuthorHouse 03/08/2024

author HOUSE

Dedicated to my husband Rich and to my three children Tyler, Owen, and Jaclyn. Thank you for always believing.

Preface

Tell me and I forget, teach me and I may remember, involve me and I will learn.
-Benjamin Franklin

This is a curious story which entices wonder for all ages. At its most primary level, this book helps children to explore shapes and images using many varieties of artistic mediums, from oil pastel, acrylic, photography, collage to watercolor and even marker. I wanted it to be visually full of textures and brilliant with color. One can find imbedded in the book, examples of primary colors with growth to a larger variety of complementary colors and of detailed types of art. This book will interest many ages, not because the art is perfect, maybe because it is not. I have seen parents point out the shapes and look for the bee on every page.

However, it is also a story of growth and of individual journey. In the beginning the art is basic then grows in complexity, much like life, depending on personal choice. Life is always about choices, right? This book explores the idea of personal choice through its use of guided visualization, sensory integration, meditation, and relaxation techniques. It is a tool that can be used as a stepping stone to helping children visualize their dreams! Once reading, imagine all the discussions to be had. I wrote this book to help children to connect with their parents in a new way. This book is a guide within a story. Parents, grandparents, teachers, siblings or even a therapist may inspire children to use known relaxation techniques, such as intentional breathing and visualization. How exciting is that!

By incorporating many types of artistic mediums, I wanted artistic freedom to expose the different perspectives of the characters. I also wanted to involve the five senses as a catalyst to the many layers of perception. I have found this book a helpful tool when a child needs to calm down, to bring in a peaceful attitude or perhaps relate to another individual. There is so much to learn from visualization and this story breaks it down to a child's level. It is really fun for kids, because they hold the power when they attempt their rainbow story!

After reading it slowly with your child, allow them to then build their own rainbow story. YOU be the guide. Help them find their own favorite scents...or tastes. Try not to pick for them. Play your child different types of music in the background as you read. Search for different sounds, if they are talking about peaches, find a peach to taste, touch, and smell!...Incorporate, incorporate, incorporate, those five senses. Please take the time to hear the words...really listen. This is a book that grows with the child. In the beginning it will entertain with vibrant colorful pictures and cute characters, when they are older you may ask them which character they identify with and why?

I am here to share with you just a piece of what I have learned on my journey...My rainbow story. My hope is that you enjoy building them also. My intention for this book is for parents to feel more connected to their children in this extremely busy technologically weighted world. Wouldn't it be great if one day during a traffic jam you ask your family, "Can I hear someone's Rainbow story today?" or you may find you want to build one for yourself.

To understand your journey, you must understand your vision.
— -Deborah James —

In Love and Hope, Deborah

On the Island of Believable there are magical horses, each named by a star which frames their eye. In the history of the land there was only one horse...one horse born with a rainbow star. This is her story...Rainbow's Story.

On a day hotter than biscuits, a very busy bee flew to the most beautiful flower patch on the island.

She was gathering only the best pollen, from the best flowers, to make the best honey. This tiny bee was of vital importance to the health of the land. She flew only during certain seasons and it was close to the end of summer. This was a busy time for the bee. The season was changing quickly.

Buzzzzzzzzz...bump.

Buzz bump,

buzz bump bump bump

"Rascals and Butterflies...I have SMACKED myself into a wall!" the bee hollered. "A HUGE BLUE WALL!" Snorting loudly as if it were trying to remove something from it's nostrils, the huge blue creature spoke, "My name is Tangerine. Am I in your way small bee?" The voice was calm and gentle.

This was very surprising to the bee. Being busy she never had time to find out about the magical star eyed horses. Now one of them was blocking her way. "I'm Sassy. Who are you calling small? And what were your parents thinking to name you Tangerine, when you are obviously some sort of INDIGO color?" The bee began repeating over and over how important her collection of pollen was and how her striped uniform was proof of her importance. The young horse found this little creature incredibly interesting.

The bee moved quickly back and forth and then back and forth again. She became very frustrated and unable to pass. "What is the rush?" said Tangerine, as she continued to block the bee by bobbing her nose up and down, then side to side.

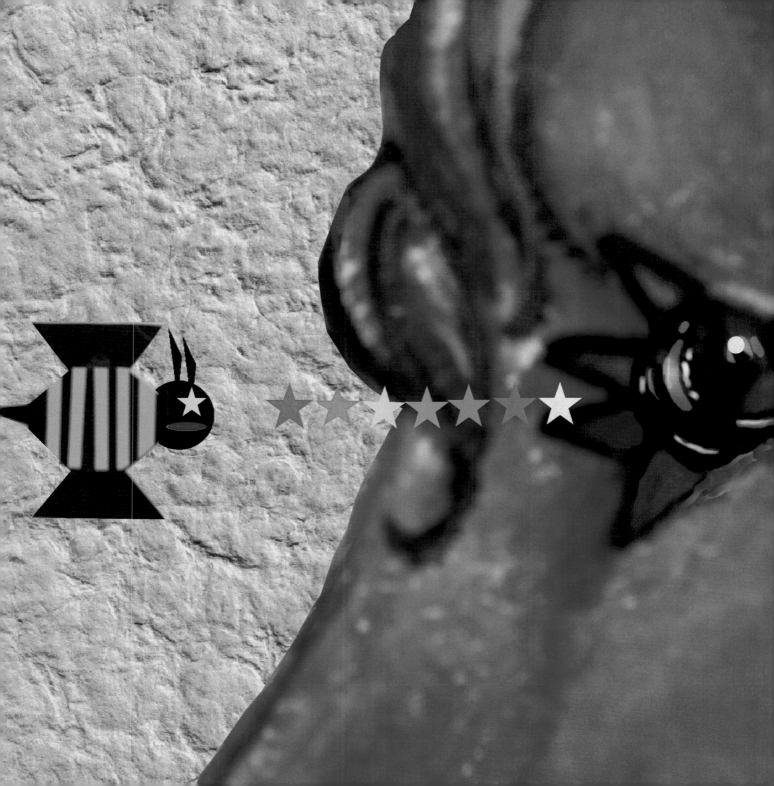

"Enjoy all these flowers. You're flying so fast.

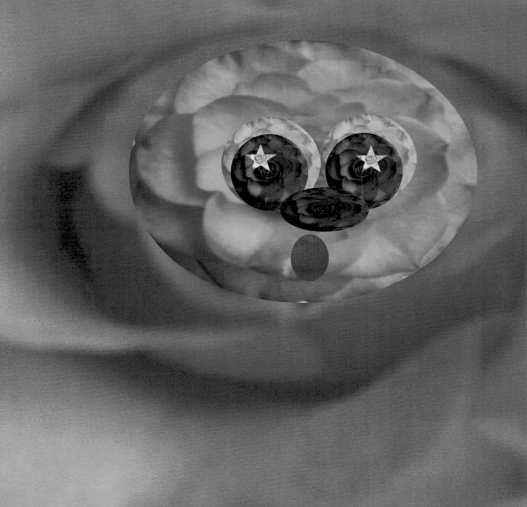

Did you know they all talk of how you tickle them? But you're gone before the first giggle."

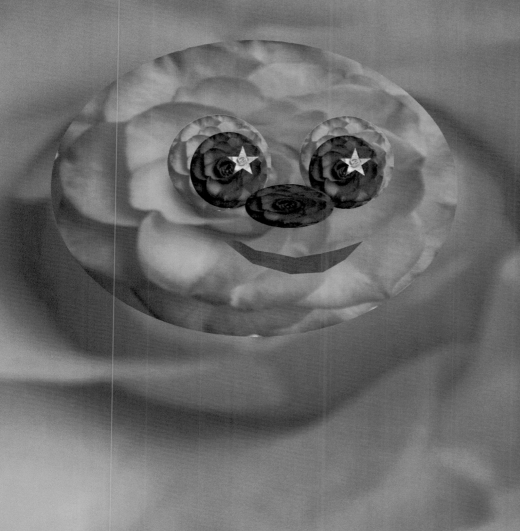

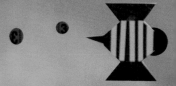

Tangerine looked at the bee with hope. Yes, yes, yes, ...Now please move your nose I must go!" Sassy was now shaking her stinger so quickly it vibrated. Tangerine had never talked with a bee before now. Their species was always too busy and fast. She was often stung by their impatience. Tangerine closed her eyes slowly to think and then suddenly popped them open. "Have you ever heard of RAINBOW'S STORY!?.... She is only the most unique horse in all the land and she was my Mama." But Sassy was gone in a flash, leaving Tangerine with a sore feeling at the tip of her nose. "STUNG AGAIN, stung again," the foal thought to herself.

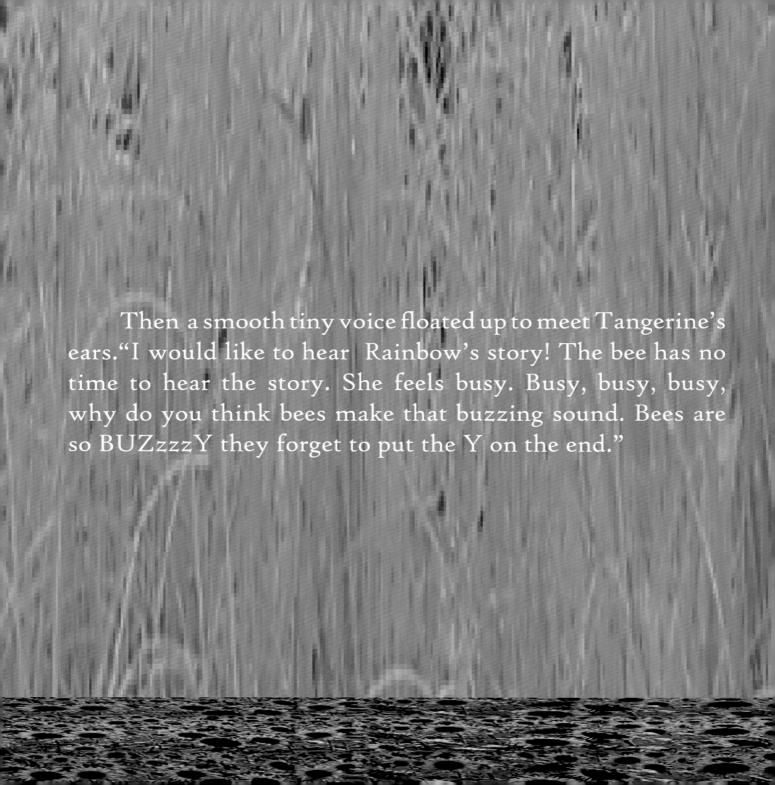

Then a smooth tiny voice floated up to meet Tangerine's ears. "I would like to hear Rainbow's story! The bee has no time to hear the story. She feels busy. Busy, busy, busy, why do you think bees make that buzzing sound. Bees are so BUZzzzY they forget to put the Y on the end."

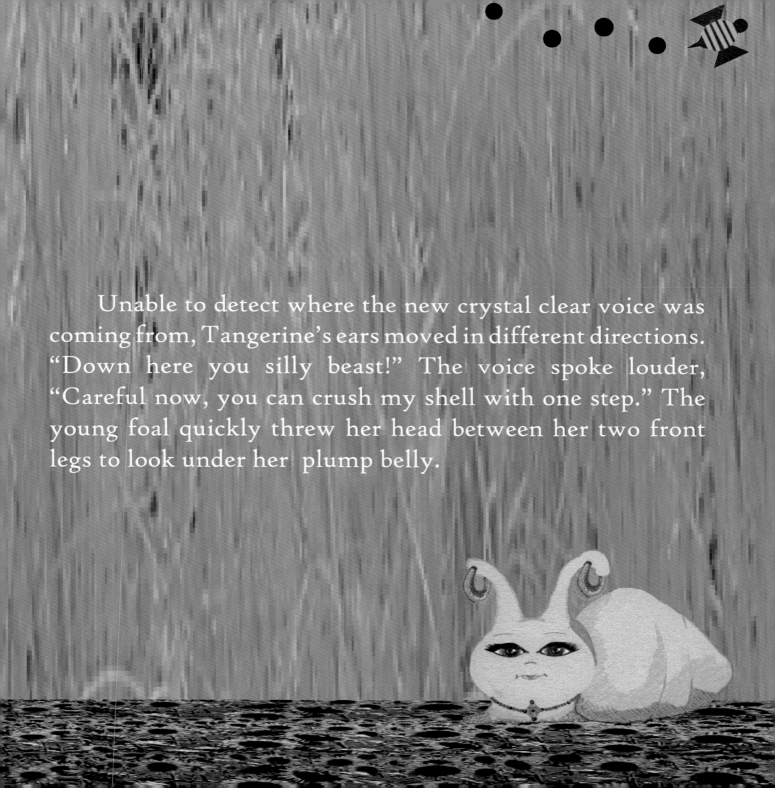

Unable to detect where the new crystal clear voice was coming from, Tangerine's ears moved in different directions. "Down here you silly beast!" The voice spoke louder, "Careful now, you can crush my shell with one step." The young foal quickly threw her head between her two front legs to look under her plump belly.

"Oh there you are... You are yellow! Really yellow and so very tiny," Tangerine was in awe. "To be honest, most think of me as a marigold color... well foofy patooty. My name is Spark. Did you know the color yellow is a hue which lands between orange and green on the color spectrum? Just in case you wanted to know the order of things, but there is much to know of the color yellow, which is why my mother named me Spark. I am special you know." Spark winked as she said special. She was mysterious and most certainly did not look like your average snail. Tangerine could feel Spark's warmth heating her belly. It was comforting.

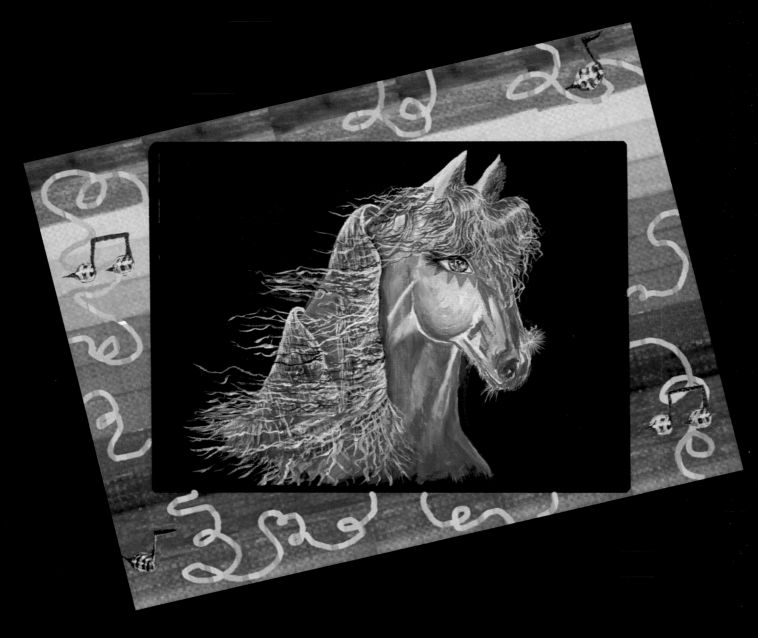

Tangerine crossed her eyes, as the small slippery snail slowly slid upon her nose. The two gazed upon each other not understanding the connection they would soon make. Spark rested as if she sat on a old comfortable chair. "Well, it is a type of story," the horse began. "My mom told me this type of story could calm me down when I became upset. It would help me explore what I enjoy and it could change every time I told it. Something about it could lead many creatures to believe in their dreams." Tangerine rolled her eyes gave a little whinny. The snail's shell appeared to be glowing a little brighter and warmer, almost electric. She looked like a little tiny light bulb glowing on Tangerine's nose. "To begin you have to find your most relaxed comfortable position and breath slowly in through your nose and out slowly from your mouth."

1.) Downward Horse

Dream

Believe

Imagine

Hope

"As you are doing this begin to imagine anything. You could imagine your family, the grass, the blue skies, or your friendships. She especially wanted me to use all of my five senses...hearing, sight, touch, taste, and smell. She would ask me to pick out my favorite time of the year and always wanted me to discuss how the story made me feel. She wanted me to use my imagination! I make one every day. This is mine for today."

Tangerine's Rainbow Story

As I walk across the field it is spring and the breeze is warm, 78 degrees. I see a rainbow beginning a few steps away. I love the orange parts the best. As I imagine moving towards the rainbow, I notice steps. There are 7 to get to the top (7 is my favorite number). When I climb to the top, I count very slowly breathing in through the nose and out through the mouth between numbers. One... Two...... Three...... Four.........

"Ok...Ok Tangerine, I get the point, I may be a snail, but I am not that slow!"

"The counting relaxes me, Spark. You are supposed to take breaths as you count each number. It helps to calm you down. My mom used the word soooooothing. Learning to do this can help you if you ever get stung by bees, bit by flies, you name it...trust me, I have tried it many times."

Once at the top of the rainbow, I imagine a field with a red barn and many colorful horses. I feel the damp, cool, green grass. There are white fences, lots of hay and oats. The oats have a very crunch nutty flavor. Sometimes I can imagine the feeling of the hay getting stuck in my teeth. It is very uncomfortable. There is a young girl with pig tails smiling by the barn. I can tell she wants to play with me. I can hear her clapping her hands and laughing.

I can smell sweet flowers. They grow on a wondrous apple tree. The apples are Granny Smith. I can taste them so tart, which gives me a little wince at the very first bite. After spending time imagining what I want to see, hear, feel, smell, and taste at the top of my rainbow, I imagine myself sliding down the rainbow with ease and grace. I feel at peace. Tangerine then opened her closed eyes with a sigh. "And that is usually when my mom would lean over to give me a kiss and wish me good night."

Rainbow's kiss to her child was the most important thing. She was filled with love and acceptance. It is why she was the most unique horse in the land of Believable. Rainbow loved everyone's stories. She believed in all of them.

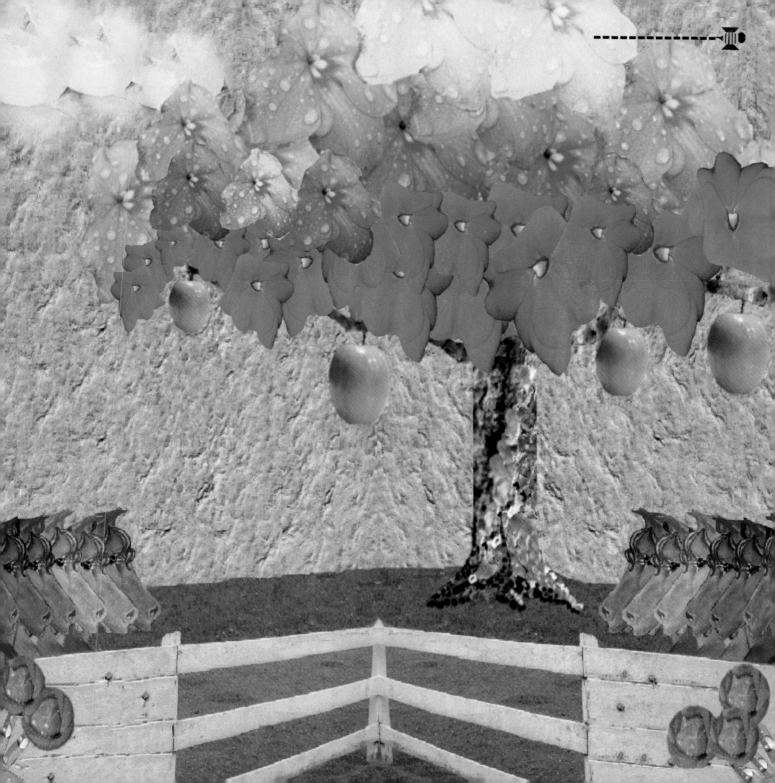

"So do you understand how to make your own story Spark? You have to imagine the story while using your five senses and you can change it anytime you tell it. Did you like mine?" The horse stood grinning ear to ear.

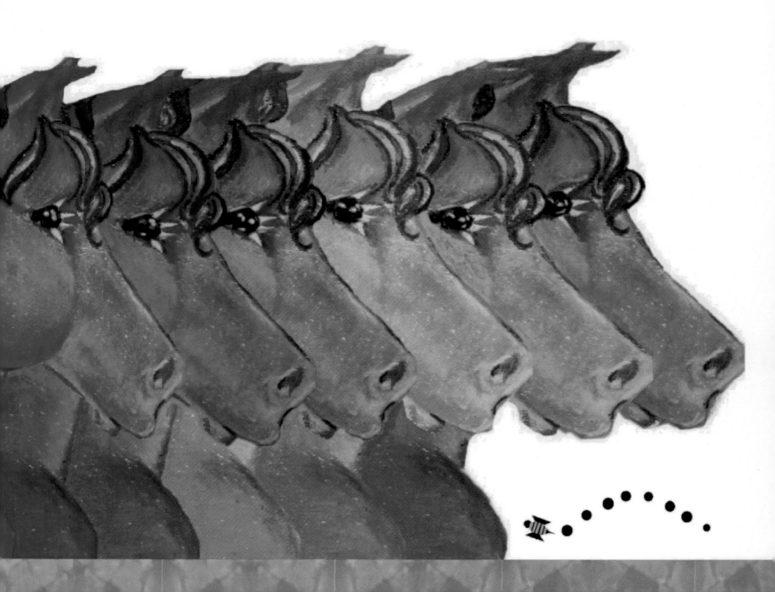

"Yes," replied the snail whose shell was now shinning all the colors of the rainbow! It was like magic. The snail looked as though she might burst out of her shell. She was completely changing. Spark asked if she could tell her rainbow story for the day. Tangerine bounced her head up and down the way horses do when they agree with you.

Imagine The Possibilities!

Spark Hardshell a Unique Vision

"It is fall, all the leaves are floating softly down all around me. I am reminded of a time when my family gave thanks for all we had received. I was thankful the turkeys didn't eat me. I see a yellow rainbow through a bunch of large oak trees. The air has a chill to it, as the sun is about to go down. When I get to my yellow rainbow, there is one step (my favorite number).

"Wait how are you going to relax with one number and one breath?" asked the young foal. "Sometimes all you need is one good breath," the snail replied. "Besides right now I think I can only handle one step."

At the top of my rainbow looking down I see nothing, but the earth. Shades of green and blue swirl around. Looking up I see a midnight blue sky changing to black with stars as far as the eyes can see.

"Nothing, but earth and space, huh?" said Tangerine feeling quite confused.

At the bottom of this rainbow, even though I can't see it now, I know I want to ride on a clear, crisp, bubbly, turquoise river. When I slide down the rainbow I feel happiness, which for me is a mix between peace and excitement. There waiting is an orange leaf for me to ride on.

"Where does the river go?... What do you see?" "I'm not sure I will have to think about it." Spark was content with not having an answer. The two of them smiled in acceptance. Spark had a fine answer. Tangerine said, "I find it interesting all I imagined was a peaceful farm, when there is a whole world out there." Spark smirked and replied, "It's a shame the bee did not have time to learn about Rainbow's Story."

Just as Spark's words rolled over her lips...

Sassy whizzed by yelling . . .

"Who said I didn't hear it?!"

The End

Printed in the United States
by Baker & Taylor Publisher Services